The Entrepreneurial Hero's Journey

Blaze your own trail

By Dave Thompson

What People Are Saying

Required reading for every single person on the planet.

Whether you're 18 or 80, every single day you're on your own hero's journey, and this manual is guaranteed to guide you on your way.

Dave has a unique way of tapping into your psyche with real world examples, helping you to gain clarity on the task at hand and the path you need to navigate to reach the promised land! Simple, thought provoking and actionable. Take action today, you won't regret it.

- L Frank

Epic read to get you along your journey

This book takes you along for a ride through the lifestyle of any hero with exceptional wisdom and clarity to empower you to navigate thru life's challenges, break past those obstacles that seem to slow you down and holds you accountable to your dreams along your way.

Choose your path and remember......its all part of the journey.

- Joshua Newton

This book delivers...and then some

Dave Thompson is the go to man when it comes to breaking your old patterns and truly 'living outrageously'. The Hero's Journey is a manifesto that promises to support you in 'blazing your own trail'. The truth is this book does more than that. In the too-the-point, no BS style Dave is well known for this book provides a powerful blue-print to breaking out of your comfort zone and living an incredible life. Powerful Reading!!

- Matt Gardner

Copyright © 2015 Thompson Coaching Group International Pty Ltd

First published in 2015

This book is a SpiritCastNetwork Book

www.spiritcastnetwork.com.au

Author: Thompson, Dave
Title: The Entrepreneurial Hero's Journey
ISBN-13: 978-1508573104
ISBN-10: 1508573107
Cover Design: Dave Thompson

For all those brave souls I meet every day out on the journey, this is for you.

May your journeys, and destinations always be fulfilling

Table of Contents

PART TWO – WISDOM, SKILLS & TOOLS OF THE HERO

A Note To The Readers

It's been over 12 months now since *"Living Outrageously – Your Hero's Journey"* was published to great success around the world. I was honored and privileged to know that readers across the world were benefiting from the philosophy of living an outrageous life.

Thanks to all my passionate followers, the book did really well, and opened up opportunities for me to travel the world, speaking and coaching and sharing my message.

Throughout my journey, a few things became clear. Firstly, the hero's journey is a model that people absolutely love. Developed first by Joseph Campbell many years ago, the model perfectly represents the journey that an early-stage entrepreneur goes. From being discontent in the old world (probably a corporate job) to finding new mentors, accepting the call to adventure and facing their deepest fears, the hero's journey encapsulates what it means to be on the entrepreneurial ride.

And, after doing a number of workshops and podcasts on the model, I knew I had to do a revised edition of this book. There was more that needed to be said on this topic.

So, this new edition, sporting a new title and sub-title, 12 new chapters of expanded content on the hero's journey, as well as new stories and examples, is targeted directly at the early stage entrepreneur, who is just getting going and wants to break free from the past so they can embrace a brand new future.

For ease of reference, the book is now in two parts – the first part takes an in-depth look at each stage of the hero's journey, while the second part provides you with the wisdom and tools and skills you will need to navigate your hero's journey.

Finally, I want to express my thanks and gratitude to you, the reader, and I want to wish you all the very best on your outrageous, entrepreneurial, hero's journey.

Dave Thompson

Raby Bay, Queensland

19 February 2015, 2.15pm

PART ONE: THE ENTREPRENEURIAL HERO'S JOURNEY

The Entrepreneurial Hero's Journey
OLD WORLD

JOURNEY HOME Ready to start next hero's journey	DISCONTENT SEARCHES FOR NEW MEETS MENTOR
DISCOVERS THE ELIXIR	REFUSES CALL ACCEPTS CALL
FACES ULTIMATE CHALLENGE	CROSSES THE THRESHOLD
Nearly dies...	ENTERS NEW WORLD

FACES TESTS, CHALLENGES & ENEMIES

CHAPTER ONE
THE OLD WORLD

"It's a funny old world"

- Margaret Thatcher

The hero is a hero; he just doesn't know it yet.

His outrageous path is right there, he just hasn't noticed it yet.

But why would he?

Everything is so calm and comfortable in his life that he believes there's nothing to worry about; now or in the future. He is following the deferred life plan (slave — save — retire) and people always tell him that he's doing great. He has a job. Probably a car. Maybe a girlfriend. "Stuff" is pretty cruisy.

Then suddenly the season of life changes, and he misses the lesson. After five years of loyal service, he gets back from lunch on Friday and to be told that he will be finishing up in a few hours. He couldn't read the sign. Or he goes in for a routine knee surgery, to come out and discover his wife left. He couldn't read the sign. Or he wakes up one day and realises he is 30kg overweight. He couldn't read the sign.

The season of life changed and he missed the turnoff. Now the creeping dread of the deferred life plan smacks him square in the face! BAM! The pain is overwhelming, and it's right up there in his business. He can't deny that a change is needed. NOW.

CHAPTER TWO

THE HERO BECOMES DISCONTENT

"Pain is inevitable, suffering is optional"

- Haruki Murakami

The Living Outrageously Hero's Journey always begins when the hero realises that something needs to change in their life. The discontent that is plaguing their current circumstances becomes too great a burden, and they decide to make plans to exit the "old world."

I've worked with clients all over the world and they all say the same thing—the old world just got so boring and mediocre that I had to do something about it. Most commonly, the story goes something like this:

"Dave, you know what? I hate my job. It's boring. I can't use my creative talents and it's not challenging me enough. I really don't care for the people I work with (except for Jimmy—we would verse each other in online poker, just to keep ourselves amused during the day… terrible, I know).

My boss doesn't give a shit and the company culture is toxic. I come home feeling stressed and drained, and that's impacting my relationship. Man, Dave! It's like you said, everyone has a case of terminal seriousness! It's as though we have to check our personalities at the door, and any laughing or having fun is prohibited!

Plus, my health is suffering. I sit down all day and get square eyes while my body is turning to mush! Nine-hour days and a two-hour commute is not a great recipe for great health! Dave, I feel this job is soul-sucking. I'm wasting my life here. I don't know what to do."

In one way or another, this person is on his way to spiritual death. The aliveness, the spirited energy of a happy human, the stoked-ness of an excited soul, is all being sucked away. Prior to this point, there might have been pain, but not enough to make them move. But now it's time. This client needs an immediate intervention to make a turning point in their life, or else risk becoming a faceless, soulless zombie… one of the living dead!

Living Outrageously Definition

"Turning Point"—*A distinct moment in time when you decide to stop living a boring life and start heading down outrageous paths.*

It's time for a Turning Point

CHAPTER THREE

SEARCHING FOR THE NEW WORLD & MEETING THE MENTOR

"There must be more to life than this"

- The Living Outrageously, Entrepreneurial Hero

The point of discontent will often set the hero off on his journey. He will begin to look for new opportunities, new ways to make money, new courses to study. Like a giraffe, his head is literally up and aware, senses tuned into the frequency of new opportunity.

This is often the point that I receive contact from a prospective new client. They are ready-ing themselves for action. The typical client interaction will go like this:

Dave:

    So, what do you want?

Client:

Well, I want the freedom and flexibility to do what I want to do. I don't want to be a slave to a desk. I don't want to sell my soul to "The Man".

Dave:

Ok, I get the bad stuff. Tell me what you <u>DO</u> want.

Client:

Well, I want to have more freedom and flexibility to do what I want. If I want to travel the world, I don't want to have to ask my boss for leave. I just want to be able to do it.

And with a little prompting, the true gold comes out of the client.

I want to be location independent, and have enough passive income coming in that I don't have to worry about my living expenses. I've thought about property and business. I want to do creative, fun work that I enjoy, so that I can help other people and make a difference.

I want to work hard, but also work smart and become wealthy so I can travel the world, go to Mount Everest Base Camp, go snorkeling in Hawaii, see bear eat salmon in Alaska, see the Northern Lights, and take the day off to see my kid's school play, or go fishing mid-week with my buddy. Or have time for sport. I want to be proud of my work and be well respected in the community, maybe even a bit of a "rock star." I want to be happy, healthy and peaceful, and have many like-minded friends.

Dave:

Great. All of that can be yours. And more. In fact, you will be surprised by how outrageous things can get. But before we begin, I need to ask you a few questions about this epic journey and making a turning point.

Client:

Sure, go ahead.

Dave:

Are you willing to face your fears and take responsibility for every result in your life?

Client:

Yes.

Dave:

Are you prepared for the tough questions; the ones that pierce through to the very being of your soul and challenge you in every way and on every level?

Are you prepared to let go of old thinking and adopt new thinking; the thinking of those who have walked this path before you?

Client:

YES.

Dave:

Are you sure?

Client:

YES! (Getting a little frustrated.)

Dave:

Are you willing to do whatever it takes to make your dreams come true? I mean, would you be prepared to sleep in your car, eat canned tuna, stay home on Friday nights, wake up early and stay up late to do tough, sometimes grueling work, talk in public, cold-call businesses, and otherwise out yourself out there to make it happen?

Client:

YES!!

Dave:

And is it okay if this process goes on for a few years? I mean, it's not like the eternal suffering of the soul-sucking deferred life plan—that lasts 40 years plus, but once you take the road to the Living Outrageously Hero's Journey, it might take a few years for you to get to your destination. You might even get lost along the way, but at least your soul will be happy because you are doing something meaningful. Is that cool?

Client:

Yeah, it is.

Dave:

And you know what? Truth be told, you might not get to your intended destination after all. But you will be able to rest easy at night, knowing you gave it a go. And that, my friend, is a destination far more worthy of satisfaction than many ever reach.

The client pauses for a moment, solemn, considering everything I have said. The next few moments of thought are critical, and will determine whether the hero even begins his journey! Some people get lost for years, even for an entire lifetime in the next stage, so read on...

CHAPTER FOUR

REFUSING THE CALL TO ADVENTURE

"No! It's not me!"

- Neo

Every hero, at some point, will refuse the call to action adventure. Always!

The clearest example of this refusal of the call comes from the hit movie, The Matrix, starring Keanu Reeves as the character Neo. In the movie, the mentor, Morpheus, comes us to Keanu while he is busy at his regular city office job. Morpheus turns to Neo and says, "You are the one (chosen to save the world), come with me". Keanu freaks out, almost ignores him and says "NO! It's not me! (I'm not the hero to save the world)".

The hero says no, because of the mental chatter, and fear. When the mentor thrusts out his hand, and says, "Follow me, I can guide you to your destination" – all sorts of stuff comes up.

"What if I'm not good enough to do this?"

"What if mum/dad/uncle Geoff find out I'm doing this?!"

It's a natural human instinct to have these protective thoughts. This is how the reptilian brain developed, and rightly so. It served to warn us against the dangers of saber-tooth tigers that could eat us in an instant. This fear is what is known as "real fear". As in, you really could die.

Except now in the modern era, such tigers are only found in history books. There is very little to actually be afraid of today, and very little that will actually kill you. You're just starting a business, man. You won't die. Be chill. Hang loose, as the Hawaiians say. Any mental chatter is what is known as "imagined fear".

Now, the truth of the matter is that many people will stay stuck in this imagined fear for years, if not a lifetime. These are the people who are all talk. And no walk. And guess what? They feel terrible inside. Knowing they are letting the fear win. It messes with your ability to trust yourself (if that's you, you will really dig Part Two – we go right into depth on how to re-build trust in self).

My best guess is that if you are reading this particular book, then you are NOT one of those people that stay stuck for a lifetime. Outrageous people tend not to let that happen! So good on you.

*AN IMPORTANT DISTINCTION: Is this path right for

you?

On the entrepreneurial hero's journey, you will be presented with all different types of paths that will seem bright and shiny. Network marketing opportunities can be particularly enticing, especially because of the connected group feeling generated at meet-ups. At times you will encounter high-pressure salesman, who put the hard word on you to sign up to their program.

In these moments, in can be easy to lose track of your own inner voice, your own inner guidance system. Sometimes, the path will resonate so vibrantly with you that you will instantly say YES and move forward. In these situations, go for it!

But other times, you will need to reflect on the prospective path ahead. Ask yourself: does this feel right for me? Do my values align with the prospective path I'm looking at? (If you don't know your values, check out Part Two of this book, where I take you through the Personal and Business Manifestos – these are statements of what you value and what's important to you on your journey.

In the end, at some point, you will have to pull the trigger and make a decision. Either Yes or No. Life is full of twists and turns, and you can always adjust your course later.

CHAPTER FIVE

ACCEPTING THE CALL TO ADVENTURE

"Say YES!!"

- Anthony Robbins

In the 2013 Hollywood movie, "The Internship", starring Vince Vaughan and Owen Wilson, there is a crucial scene that really kick-starts the action. Having just been fired from their sales jobs, Owen Wilson takes up a lower paying, uninspiring job selling beds in a furniture store.

The furniture storeowner is berating him when his buddy Vince walks into the store, brimming with enthusiasm! He has just found an opportunity for them to do an internship at Google! After refusing the call to adventure for quite a few minutes (saying all the usual stuff like "oh what a silly idea", "they will never pick us", "I've got bills to pay, man!"), Owen's furniture store boss walks in again and berates him, again. At this point, the pain of not taking action becomes too much, and Owen accepts the call to adventure, saying the famous words "I Quit!" and storming out with Vince, heading for their destiny!

This scenario is a great example of how the entrepreneurial hero eventually accepts the call. After refusing the call initially, the pain then gets piled up so high he can't take it anymore, and he accepts the call. Only at this point can he truly "Say YES!" and begin the real work on the path.

In my hero's journey, it took me 7 years of refusing the call to adventure, before finally the pain got too much, and I accepted the call. I'd been studying at law school, and knew from the first day that I didn't want to be a lawyer. I was discontent with the thought of a lifetime as a lawyer, and so began searching for new.

In my search, I had many entrepreneurial adventures – I dabbled in boat detailing, I started a web design business, I sold hand made cricket bats on EBay and even imported rock climbing shoes from China. I'd met mentors, but none had really resonated with me.

Truth was, I was not REALLY committed. I had one foot in

law, and the other foot in business. This was me existing in that "imagined fear" space that I mentioned earlier. Accepting the call to adventure is really a definitive START/STOP moment in time, when you cut off other possibilities (burning the boats, as they say) and say yes to your hero's journey.

This might mean signing up to a course, starting new study, moving cities, ending a relationship, or dissolving a previous business. It could also mean quitting your job. It's when you say to yourself:

I am worth it!
I am worth more!!
I can play a bigger game!!!
This is more to me than what the world is seeing right now!!!!
My destiny awaits!!!!!

When this happens, clients turn to me and say:

Client:

      Dave, let's do this. I'm ready. Let's go!!

It's time to enter the new world.

But first, the hero must cross the threshold...

CHAPTER SIX

CROSSING THE THRESHOLD

"Put your big boy pants on, it's going to be wild!"

- Lachlan Ferguson

Put yourself in the shoes of Dorothy, from the world famous movie, "The Wizard Of Oz". She had just accepted the call to adventure to find the Wizard, of Oz, and before she knows it, she is in this incredible tornado! The tornado swirls around and around, it's wild, it's crazy and there certainly is a high level of exhilaration.

Do you remember what Dorothy sees while she is in the tornado? She sees her Old World, and her New World. There's her uncle, her mum, her dog Toto – all from her hometown in Kansas. Then there's the wicked witch of the west, plus a whole heap of other new things. The old and the new are swirling round, and it's quite crazy for a while there!

This is the hero crossing the threshold.

For the entrepreneur, crossing the threshold begins as soon as the decision has been made to accept the call to action. As soon as you say yes to that program, as soon as you decide fully to commit and take action, then you are officially in the threshold.

Let me give you an example. A client of mine was in a business with 2 other partners. After much discontent with the partnership, she finally decided to dissolve it, and go out on her own. She made the decision, and then it took 2 months for all the legal and accounting matters to be finalized. It was a bit wild there for a while, as disputes were raised and settled. At one point, in the heat of the moment when resolving a legal matter, she said to me "What have I got myself into?!" This is quite normal when you are crossing the threshold. When transitioning from old world to new world, you can quite reasonably expect to feel exhilarated, with a "hold onto your panties" type feeling!

Another client quit his job, and started a consultancy business. He complained about being emotionally unstable as soon as he decided to quit his job. When he realized he was just crossing the threshold, he regained his certainty and was able to begin making more decisions that would ultimately lead him forward on his path.

Now, if you want to progress fast through the threshold, so you can get to the New World and experience all it's wonder and colour, the best advice is to make decisions.

Getting caught in the threshold is not a place you want to be.

So keep deciding, because decisions help you to move forward, into the new world.

CHAPTER SEVEN

ENTERING THE NEW WORLD

"It's a whole new world"

- Aladdin

Can you imagine being in the audience in 1939, when the Wizard of Oz movie first premiered in cinemas? Can you imagine the surprise, the awe and amazement the audience must have experienced when Dorothy popped out the other side of the black and white tornado, and landed in the full colour yellow brick road?! It must have been magical! And so exciting!

Full vibrant colour! For the first time! And a yellow brick road! And plenty of new friends! Munchkins, nonetheless! And, a path to follow – the yellow brick road.

This is the excitement that many new entrepreneurs feel during the first 30 days of their hero's journey in the new world. I say 30 days, because in my experience, that's how long the "honeymoon period" lasts.

The hero has said yes to themselves and their outrageous life, but he has no idea what he has *really* gotten himself into. He is yet to fully appreciate the enormity of the journey ahead! He doesn't know what it takes to run a business, be an elite athlete, or be a star. And if he did, he probably would have never started the journey.

The hero is now beginning to realise that the turning points happen everyday, with every decision he makes.

CHAPTER EIGHT

SIDENOTE: THE HERO BECOMES A REBEL

"Crush It!"

- Gary Vaynerchuk

This stage is also where you see the hero adopt a rebellious, "fuck you, get out of my way" attitude. In his mind, the old world has done him wrong by leading him down the wrong path, and now he has the power. Everyone is going to see just how powerful he is!!

The hero's behaviour might make him reckless, and he may become aggressive or even act wantonly. He might:

• Immediately quit his job because he is sick of working for "the man".

• Start up a new business with no money, talent, or skills at his disposal.

• Go to Vegas and party like crazy, spending all his hard-earned savings.

None of this behaviour is good or bad. It just is. Behaviour. Something to be aware of. Because this rebellious state can be quite functional, but it can also be dysfunctional.

The functional rebellious hero gets shit done. He forces and creates change. Very quickly. There is no hesitation as he attacks his journey with vigour, breaking through and running as far away from the site of his original pain as possible. He might even begin to rally people to his cause and start a movement that is fighting for a worthwhile change.

This type of hero has forgiven the people responsible for the hurts of the past, but he is still angry about it.

The contrast is the dysfunctional rebel who has not forgiven the hurts of the past, and acts out to spite the people who hurt him.

The rebellious stage is often useful to get the hero moving, in order to overcome inertia.

CHAPTER NINE

FACING TESTS, CHALLENGES & ENEMIES

"Do the work"

- Steve Pressfield

In the movie The Matrix, the hero – Neo – spends a significant amount of time in this stage of the hero's journey. He undergoes intense training - both physical, mental and emotional as he prepares for his ultimate challenge, that of saving the world.

Starting your own business can seem like a thick jungle you have never penetrated. You have no idea where to go, little idea about what will work, and are really in survival mode. Having a guide on your team, someone who has been through the jungle before, will be of huge assistance to you. The guide can tell you to stay away from the sinking sand, take the north route by the swamp, and stay silent when you see a bear. Now, you're not literally in the jungle, but you can see the value in having a coach or mentor to help you navigate the challenges.

One of the biggest advantages of a coach is that they know "what" you need to focus on, in order to progress fast. They have the strategies to get you the results you want in the shortest period of time. (If you are excited about learning how to model excellence and get super fast results, stay tuned for Part Two of this book where we go into depth on how to model the best of the best.)

This stage of the hero's journey is often about rolling up your sleeves, and doing the work. It is also known as "paying your dues". No one was ever an overnight success, except after 10 years of work, turning up, day after day, to learn and get better. The hero must carry with him the spirit of continuing on, always, even in the face of no results.

Clients often ask me what it takes to be a success in business. My simplest, and punchiest answer is, "Do something worth talking about". Like Seth Godin says, build a purple cow. Build something remarkable. That is truly the work of the hero.

During the epic years of the #1 iTunes Living Outrageously Podcast, co-host Matt Kelly and I were known for being very outside the box characters. We did anything we could to bring personality and pizazz to the show – we sampled exotic herbal teas, brought our favourite foods (coconuts) on the air, and one night, we even did a crazy psychedelic dub-step dance! These events created remarkable stories, gained us a big reputation for being guys who truly lived outrageously.

So, what remarkable thing you could do right now in your business?

The other benefit of doing remarkable things is that it's a clear opt-in, or opt-out for your followers in the marketplace. When they see who you truly are, they will either love it, or say it's not for them. This dynamic of "in or out" is one of the key challenges the hero faces in the entrepreneurial journey. Who is in your tribe?

The tests, challenges and enemies stage is also a stage of experimentation. In business, you need to interact with the market to get feedback on your offerings. Matt Kelly is a genius at this. His creativity knows no bounds. One time, when promoting an industry networking event, he had his staff "hijack" two life-size toy pigs, and created a whole social media following for the event – all because of soft, furry toy pigs. His experiment led him to much insight into the networking event, and how to take it to the next level, next time they host that event.

So, what could you experiment with, right now?

This stage of facing tests and challenges, and overcoming enemies, can take a number of months or even years in business. With each test, the hero hones his skills, stepping up to each challenge and facing what he needs to face. As time progresses, there will come a time when the hero is ready. Either he will feel that something big is coming, or his mentor will tell him it is time. The hero may not consciously realize, but the journey home is just starting. His ultimate challenge is on the horizon, and he must step forward with courage and bravery, for his skills are about to be tested, and failure could be fatal!

CHAPTER TEN

FACING THE ULTIMATE CHALLENGE

"Hope is not a strategy, luck is not a factor, fear is not an option"

- James Cameron

Having journeyed so far, the hero is now about to face the ultimate challenge, where he could potentially face death or destruction. He will need all his skills, training, knowledge, talent and abilities to break through, conquer the challenge, and rise up to the next level.

Think about the recent hit movie series The Hunger Games, with Jennifer Lawrence starring as the hero, Katniss. In each of those movies, she faces a number of tests and challenges, learns who her enemies are (the people in the Capitol) before facing the final, ultimate challenge which could result in her death. In the first movie in the series, the ultimate challenge is the moment where Katniss and Peter are the last two people alive in the game. The rules say that only one can finish victorious (e.g. alive). So Katniss finds some poison berries, and agrees with Peter that they will both eat the berries at the same time. Her quick wit and fast thinking allow her to outsmart the game, and overcome the ultimate challenge, just when she was about to die.

The same thing happens in the second Hunger Games movie, where Katniss, facing death, again, manages to fire an arrow at the force field and shut it down – just when everyone was about to die! This time she had allies on her side – the other members of the game, who helped her come up with the plan.

And so it is with the entrepreneurial hero's journey. There will be times where it will exceptionally difficult, and the hero will be called upon to demonstrate all his skills and talents, or else face destruction.

You might face a cash flow crisis, and have to hustle in sales that day to keep the dream alive.

You might hold a big event, that if successful, will skyrocket your progress during the next 12 months in business.

You might be involved in a lengthy negotiation, that if handled correctly, could open up international opportunities for your business.

The ultimate challenge can take many forms, and one cannot

say exactly what form it will come in for you. But one thing is for sure, you will face it. And when you do, the advice is simple. You absolutely must go all in. 100% all in. With every ounce of strength, wit, heart and soul, give everything you have got. Leave it all out on the field. There is always a way. You just need to find it.

CHAPTER ELEVEN

DISCOVERING THE ELIXIR

"Sweet are the fruits of adversity"

- Shakespeare

Having overcome the ultimate challenge, and survived, the hero is now left with the elixir. In the hero's journey, the elixir is the special knowledge and understanding that comes from facing the ultimate challenge, and surviving.

It is the moment of realization. It is the moment of clarity. It is the moment of truth.

It is the moment when all else fades away, and the hero connects to himself and what's true for him. It is when he realizes he didn't need to "be" someone else to get the job done. It's when he reconnects with the things most important to him in life – his family, his friends, his home.

Having faced death, everything is now in perspective. It is at this point, that the hero leaves behind old behaviors that did not serve him well during the ultimate challenge. For example, he may leave behind crippling emotions of fear, doubt and guilt. Further, old stories about what is possible may also fall away.

The hero has just proven to himself the extraordinary potential that lies inside of him, and so this really is a time of re-birth. New possibilities are everywhere, and the hero may notice a stillness he has not experienced for some time. This is a time for reflection, and learning because soon, the hero will be on his journey home.

CHAPTER TWELVE

THE JOURNEY HOME

"Remember kid, there's heroes and there's legends. Heroes get remembered but legends never die, follow your heart kid, and you'll never go wrong."

- Babe Ruth

Now with the elixir, the hero can return home. He might physically return to his old world home, like Dorothy going back to Kansas. Or he might re-enter the old world, like Neo did in the Matrix. Or, he might face the same old problem he was facing when he left the old world originally. Except this time, it's not a problem anymore, because he has overcome the challenges and learnt what he needed to learn.

For the entrepreneurial hero, the journey home may literally be a trip home from an overseas business meeting. Or it might involve returning to his team, and sharing his new knowledge with them.

This stage of the hero's journey has the themes of sharing, reconnection, peace and harmony. It's like the calm after the storm. There still may be some tidying up to do, after the ultimate challenge, but the main challenge has been overcome.

Hero's who have gone out on their own and started their own business may find this moment particularly rewarding. Often the hero will leave the Old World because everyone is working a job, and the hero can't stand a job! So he leaves the Old World, searching for new. After undergoing his hero's journey, he can often now return to the Old World, but this time carrying a new inner peace, contentment, and results. He can then share his experiences with his friends from the Old World, and potentially be an inspiration to them, lighting a fire within them to embark on their own hero's journey.

And this is how the hero becomes a legend.

The legend is the character that has gone on so many hero's journeys that he is almost like folklore. Consider the legends of our day in sport. Season after season, they face their ultimate challenge, and so, as Jimmy Barnes sung, "become legends of their time."

Legends inspire the greatness within us all. They provide a role model, someone to look up to for guidance and inspiration. I sense that if you are reading this book, you too want to become a legend of your space. Not so much for personal glory (although that will happen, and is rather nice to be acknowledged), but so you can inspire others.

Because ultimately, isn't that why you took the hero's journey in the first place? To help yourself, sure, but mostly to help others unleash the hero within them.

PART TWO: WISDOM, SKILLS & TOOLS OF THE HERO

Now that you know how the hero's journey works, the second part of this book gives you the tools you will need as you set out to become a hero.

Enjoy J

CHAPTER THIRTEEN
STAND UP FOR WHAT YOU BELIEVE IN

OVERCOMING REJECTION

Now that you've made a change, it's time for your first challenge and lesson! There is a strong chance that the people around you—family, friends, work colleagues—will try to impose their beliefs on you. Announcing that you want to quit your job as a highly paid lawyer to travel the world, while helping people and playing sport, will often trigger that.

"You can't make money out of that!" they'll say.

"Uncle Bob did that and look at him now! He's broke."

"That will never work!"

"You enrolled in what?!"

This can be very hard to take initially, because belonging to and being part of the tribe is probably still very important to you. You've moved out of the spiritual death situation, but have not yet transitioned into that new world outrageous identity you'd like to be. And that's okay, because it is coming.

In the meantime, the rejection you feel when family and friends impose their beliefs upon you can seem very real. The family tribe and culture you come from may have quite prescriptive rules about what you need to do in order to be deemed successful and loved. It probably looks something like this:

> Go to school and get good grades.
>
> Do the same in college.
>
> Get a good job, probably as a doctor, lawyer, accountant, engineer.
>
> Save, get a mortgage, work hard.
>
> Retire at 65, if you can.
>
> All stuff you "should" do.

Curiously—and of critical importance to the success of the Living Outrageously Hero's Journey —the hero doesn't accept these cultural myths of "seemingly truth." He sees these comments for what they are—desperate cries for you to be careful. They are scared you will get hurt.

See, in caveman times, if you left the tribe and went out on your own, the heads of the tribe would have every reason to feel scared for you—what if you got lost, or injured, or a bear attacked you, or an eagle came bombing down and attacked your eye? All of these things were quite likely to happen.

In the modern world today, about the worst thing that can happen is that you will run out of money and have to get a job again, e.g. you are back where you started.

Your family and friends mean well, because they are scared for you. After all, what you are attempting to do is outrageous.

ACTIVITY: WHAT TO DO

1. See it for what it is. They care for you and they love you. They are scared for you.

2. Ask, is it true that everyone, all of the time, fails at that?

3. Realise it's not true.

4. Thank them for their concern and let them know you love them.

5. Go get results. Not for their approval, but for you.

If it's really burdensome to listen to their story, don't tell them what you are doing. A dog only barks at something it doesn't understand. If they don't know, they won't bark. When the journey is well in progress or complete, the results will speak for themselves.

6. Repeat as often as necessary.

THE IMPORTANCE OF YOUR OWN PERSONAL MANIFESTO

Often we take on the values and beliefs of those people closest to us—our parents. The hallucination is that we have to behave and believe what they believe in order to receive their love. Failure to follow them will mean failure to receive the love we crave. It can certainly seem that way until we remember that we are loved just by being.

So, with that in mind, it's time to develop your own Personal Manifesto—the things that you believe and value and the things you will stand up for. These are ideas about the way you will live, and how you will make decisions. It's not a crappy corporate 'missions and values' that gets rehashed at the company retreat and then never touched again. This is highly personal to you and represents the values and ideals that you stand for.

> It makes it easy to say yes or no at every turning point.
>
> It allows you to stay true to your journey.
>
> It helps you make quality decisions.
>
> It helps people to know whether to buy your product.

What exactly is a Personal Manifesto?

It's simply a half page to two pages of ideas about what your life stands for, and it's written in your own language. For example, my friend Matt Kelly ate dirt as a kid, and one day he went online and broadcast that fact to the thousands of viewers of The Living Outrageously Podcast. He firmly believes in a world of no judgment. Instead of writing, "I believe in not judging people," he used his own words and wrote, "If you ate dirt as a kid, that's cool with me."

At a fundamental level, the Living Outrageously Manifesto is this:

> *We believe that you can lead an outrageous life, whatever that means for you.*
>
> *To live this outrageous life, you must stand up for what you believe in.*
>
> *Impossible is an opinion, despite what others tell you.*
>
> *There is always a strategy that will get you the result right now, not later.*
>
> *The aim is to enjoy a full experience of life, by helping the world to be a better place and by enjoying the plentiful bounties the world has to offer.*

As you can see, by stating what I believe in upfront and making it as clear as day, people know whether to opt in or opt out when they see me. They either love it and are in, or they don't like it yet and are out. There is no mediocre middle ground of wasting each other's time. We are not being beige here. As Zig Ziglar said, "This is the zig when everyone is zagging."

MONEY IN THE BANK: BUSINESS MANIFESTO

Imagine the profound impact this will have on your business. In a sea of same-same providers, your clear statement about your values and ideals allows your customers to easily pick you out of a crowd.

Imagine you are an accountant, massage therapist, web developer, or engineer and you go down to the local market with all the other accountants. Each of you has a sign with "Accountant" written on it. When the day begins and customers come walking past you, how else would they pick you out of the crowd? You are the same beige as every one else! This is where standing up for what you believe in becomes hugely important.

Simon Sinek argues that people buy why you do your thing, not what you do. They can get the "what" from anyone. That's because in today's society, it has to be so important to really care.

When you really care, this is when you really start to live outrageously.

DO YOU REALLY CARE?

As you progress along your own journey of living outrageously, you will meet others who are on a similar path. You'll notice that so many of them are awesome at talking a big game. Some may even say that they genuinely do care. But when you take a closer look, very few are actually walking their talk. Few will actually have the burning desire to do whatever it takes to fulfill their journey and mission. They care when it's convenient, but don't care so much when it is not.

This is where the true heart and soul of the leader—the Living Outrageously hero—is revealed. When things get hard, when the chips are down and your back is against the wall and you have just been knocked down 25 times in a row, will you still care enough to get up and do the right thing?

If you can say yes to this, then an outrageous life awaits you. Congratulations!

DOES YOUR BUSINESS REALLY CARE?

Companies that are willing to go the extra mile for their customers and provide a WOW! service and experience will be the only ones left serving as the 21st century progresses. As globalisation takes off, and your product or service can be outsourced and performed offshore for 1/10 the cost of a local provider, why should a customer employ you? Increasingly, the only way to win and gain a raving fan customer will be to care more about them than anyone else.

GIVE-A-CRAP MARKETING

Zappos.com is a great example of a company that cares. They are an online shoe retailer run by CEO Tony Sheih. Customer service staff will go to extraordinary lengths to assist their customers, even going as far as to order pizza for their customer on the phone. The customer didn't end up buying any shoes, but the incredible word of mouth they generated because of this action was priceless. Well, not actually priceless. Amazon bought Zappo for $1 billion.

Gary Vaynerchuk, in his book *Thank You Economy*, says that in this modern online world, he who cares most will win.

You've got to care more than your competitor.

ACTIVITY: CREATE YOUR OWN PERSONAL & BUSINESS MANIFESTO

This should be about half a page to two pages of short ideas that you are willing to stand up for. I encourage you to write freely and openly, and to use your own words, especially unique things you say. Don't be afraid to include quite personal or seemingly socially inappropriate stuff.

For example, I have a client who is a weightlifting surfer, who makes a living as a musician. Before every musical performance, he whispers to himself, "YOU THE MAN!"

To create your own manifesto, try finishing these:

Life is…

People are…

I am…

Fun is…

I can…

Love is…

Health is…

Happiness is…

I am quirky because…

This should get you started and be enough to kick-start your own personal manifesto.

CHAPTER FOURTEEN
IMPOSSIBLE IS AN OPINION

"There is always a way, every time in every situation."

- Dave Thompson

Other people will be quick to place limits on what they think you can achieve. The hero on the Journey to Living Outrageously knows that there is always a way to achieve anything you want, and pursues it with relentless vigour. He knows that he can and will triumph against the odds, and despite all obstacles. He knows the pain of not giving it a go will last far longer than the temporary pain he faces on the path to his goal. That's why he musters up all his courage, creativity, playfulness and flare, and charges forward into the unknown— backing himself all the way.

BACK YOURSELF

In early 2010, after yet another injury, my dream of one day playing rugby for Australia seemed lost. I was injured, unfit and unhappy. At 24 years of age, by almost every account, I had missed my chance at the big time. In a time of reflection one day, I asked myself if I really wanted to represent Australia in rugby, or if it was just that I wanted the pride and satisfaction of wearing the green and gold.

The answer was that I wanted to represent Australia regardless of the sport.

So that prompted another question: "What sport do I have the best chance of making it elite in the shortest period of time?" Sports like weightlifting, powerlifting, Olympic and freestyle wrestling all came up. Then I remembered how one of my mentors, Tim Ferris, had won the USA National Taiwanese Kickboxing after taking up the sport six weeks prior. I began to think obscure.

Handball.

Handball (**not** the 4-square tennis ball schoolyard version) is an emerging sport in Australia, but absolutely huge in Europe. With the help of Mr Google, the sport of beach handball come onto the radar, and training was the next night!

After just two training sessions, I decided that this sport would be my target. It could give me an Australian jersey, and if my preparation was good, I might get a place in the team for the Beach Handball World Championships in Oman in 2012.

I had 18 months before selections. 18 months to become an elite player in a sport.

I had never played before. The obstacles were enormous.

I had no idea how to play the game. So I bought match tapes, and dissected their strategy and modeled their technique.

I had no idea how to do 360-degree spin shots (a crucial part of the game). So I went to ballerina and trampolining and gymnastics schools to learn how.

My injured right shoulder made it almost impossible to throw. So I found one of the world's best ART therapists, Pedro Alcobio, who fired me up.

When I moved back to Brisbane just a month later, I had no team and no competition in which to learn, practice and develop. So I started my own tournament, Redlands Beach Handball. On a sloped beach where the water covered half the court at high tide, it was far from ideal. But with some goal posts made by my brother, we played for 50 consecutive weeks, eventually taking two teams to the Australian Championship in

2012.

And, as if we had not faced enough obstacles already, the hotel we were staying at tried to evict us on the night before the final Australian team selections. As the dust settled on the final afternoon, the selections read out the team to go to the world championship:

Nick Thompson – Redlands Beach Handball

Ben Dawson – Redlands Beach Handball

Dave Thompson – Redlands Beach Handball

I'd made it. Along with my brother, Nick, and another Redlands player. The impossible had been made possible.

TRUST SELF TO EXECUTE

For so many of the clients I work with, not backing themselves is at the core of the issue. They have been trodden on, trampled on and crushed so many times that their self-confidence is shattered. Their ability to complete even seemingly simple tasks has vanished because they can't trust themselves to execute such a task, especially when the going gets tough. And, with the modern proliferation of electronic devices and modern conveniences such as food and alcohol to distract them, it's easy to see how they end up sad and frustrated with their lack of results.

Backing yourself is the key to the hero succeeding in his outrageous journey. The task might seem impossible, but if he backs himself and stands firm in his personal manifesto, the impossible becomes possible.

REBUILD TRUST IN YOURSELF

Sometimes part of the hero's journey involves learning how to trust your own ability once again. This can appear to be a daunting task, especially for those who have experienced repression and oppression. But, there is a way out. And it involves recreating your reference points for success. You can be successful at the most of simple tasks, such as brushing your teeth.

Imagine that the hero's goal is to lose 30kg. It seems impossible, as he's tried every diet and exercise plan under the sun. He set himself the goal of eating healthy and exercising for one hour a day, five days a week. But, after a successful first day, he then quits on the second day and beats himself up for being a failure, and feels guilty because he couldn't follow through, again!

So, this is what he must do:

ACTIVITY: SUPERCHARGE THE REBUILDING OF TRUST

1. Pick a tiny task, perhaps brushing your teeth, picking up the groceries, or going for a five-minute walk.

2. Complete that task like a BOSS! Do it to the absolute best of your ability.

3. Pick a slightly larger task and repeat.

If ever there was a magic formula, this is it. I wish it were more complicated. But it's not.

Day by day, hour-by-hour, as you complete tasks, you will gain a new reference point for successfully completing the task. Your confidence will grow. Bit by bit, you'll be able to move on to bigger and bigger goals as you gradually regain trust in your ability.

A mentor of mine, Sharon Pearson, once called it "sneaking up on success." Don't try and eat the whole elephant in one bite— nibble at him. So, go and make that first $1 in your online business, help just one person, walk for just one minute, or be happy for just one hour. That's how an outrageous life starts.

FOCUS ON FINDING THE WAY

The success of the hero's outrageous life is built on the fundamental step of focusing his attention on finding the way.

I did the complete opposite for seven years.

> "I don't want to go to law school."
>
> "I don't want to be a lawyer."
>
> "I don't want to work for the man."

And what happened?

> I went to law school.
>
> I became a lawyer.
>
> I worked for the man.

The hero knows that in an unpredictable environment, there are many things beyond his control. Chaos ensues, and yet he also knows that he controls one supremely powerful weapon—focus.

WHAT YOU FOCUS ON IS WHAT YOU GET

I learned my lesson of focus the hard way. My focus was directed at NOT going to law school, but I kept finding myself drawn to it. That's because your brain doesn't understand negative commands.

- I don't want to be late è You want to be late!

- I don't want to be fat è You want to be fat!

- I don't want to be broke è You want to be broke!

So many clients I see make this fundamental error of focus. They are brilliant at telling me how bad things are, but are not very clear on exactly what they do want!

Your life can transform in a moment, if you just swing your laser focus onto the outrageous path.

YOUR FOCUS IS PRECIOUS

Famous researcher Mihaly Csikszentmihalyi, in his book *Flow*, discovered that at any one moment, you have over two million pieces of sensory information coming at you. Our human brains would be overwhelmed if we needed to process all two million pieces at once. So, we filter the information based on what is important to us, and what we believe or don't believe.

This filtration process leaves us with between 5 and 9 chunks of information. So, if you can only focus and process about seven things at once, doesn't it make sense to only focus on the things you want?

THE AUSCHWITZ SURVIVOR

A brilliant, inspiring tale of focus and finding the way.

Hans (not his real name) was a Polish author captured by the Nazis in World War 2. While his wife and daughters were taken to another concentration camp, he was taken to the most infamous of them all, Auschwitz.

In the miserable cold of the Polish winter, he was taken into the camp with all the other prisoners, in a large truck. While he was fortunate to not be immediately gassed to death on entry, he began to appreciate the grim reality of life as a prisoner at Auschwitz.

There was very little warm clothing, very little food, and the Nazis treated the prisoners violently. As the days of winter began to pass, Hans noticed people dying around him. Rapidly. He realised he had to escape or die trying, and secretly began to talk to other prisoners about developing a plan. But the others had all given up. They said things like, "There is no way we can escape!" "What's the point?", "You couldn't even if you tried." and "Where would you go and what would you do when you got out?"

Their seven chunks of information were focused on pain or how they couldn't do it. And so, understandably, they began to give up hope and die. But not Hans. He made it his mission to find a way to escape, despite the seemingly insurmountable odds. He directed all seven chunks of his precious focus towards finding an escape plan and, after several days of looking, he finally discovered a way that he thought might just work.

Every afternoon after the gas baths had just killed over 100 people, the Nazis would drag the dead, naked bodies out of the gas chamber and pile them up while they waited for the morgue truck that would take the bodies to an external gravesite.

Hans saw opportunity. He acted that day. Straight after the bodies had been piled up outside the gas chamber, Hans stripped off, lay down, and pretended to be dead.

Hours passed and Hans was getting really cold, but finally the guards came and threw Hans into the morgue truck. The other bodies squished in around him and it was tough to breathe, but Hans was determined that this would be the way to his freedom.

In the dark of night, Hans and the bodies finally arrived at the gravesite and were unloaded. Buried under the weight of so many bodies, Hans struggled to breathe. But he knew that he was close now.

He waited what felt like hours, until he was sure the truck was gone for good. When he was sure enough to make a move, he climbed up out of the bodies and literally ran for his life. No clothes, no shoes, and in the freezing cold. Hans ran for ten miles in the dark before finally coming to a small town he was familiar with and found shelter in an abandoned house.

He had found his freedom!

IMPOSSIBLE IS AN OPINION. THERE IS ALWAYS A WAY. NO MATTER WHAT THEY SAY.

ACTIVITY: LASER TARGET YOUR FOCUS

Take a moment to notice the language that you use. Are you focused on what you want or what you don't want? What could you do to filter your experience so that you experience the results you want? What could add to your focus?

CHAPTER FIFTEEN
ZERO TO HERO

"Why use the slow lane when there's a fast lane?"

- Anonymous

EVERYTHING IS A STRATEGY

The hero knows that everything, absolutely everything, he does is a strategy—one that either leads him to a result that he likes or a result that he doesn't. And since the hero is on his journey to living outrageously, it is the fast lane—the zero to hero in the shortest period of time—strategies that the hero is most interested in.

A strategy is like a recipe. Add together particular ingredients in a particular sequence and get a specific result. Mix together two eggs, flour, milk and pour into a tray to bake at 180 degrees for two hours—and you'll see the result of a cake. Change or tweak any of those ingredients and you will get a different result.

Imagine baking those ingredients for 12 hours.

Some very common deferred life plan strategies go something like this:

Go to school Study hard (12 years)		Go to college Get a good job (6 years)		Work hard and save (40 years)		Usually, a safe comfortable, middle-class lifestyle
	+		+		=	
			+	Get mortgage		
			+	Get married		

Now, there isn't anything wrong with this. There isn't any judgment around the use of this strategy. Many people are happy using this strategy. My only question to you is, how is that strategy working for you?

If you're reading this book right now, my guess is that you want more. You want to live outrageously, whatever that means to you. You don't want to settle for second best. You want to find someone who has achieved your desired result, and you want to do what they did. Because, after all, the age-old saying still applies here: Do the same thing you have always done and continue to get the results you have always gotten!

So, as you embark on your Living Outrageously Hero's Journey, it is vital that you are aware of the three major strategies that have the power to literally stop your mission in its tracks.

THE 3 SHOW-STOPPERS AND WHAT TO DO ABOUT THEM

THE PERFECTIONIST STRATEGY

You might know someone who does this. Everything has to be perfect. They run around all day, striving for perfection, but never quite get there, or, if they do, it's only temporary.

> They quadruple triple check documents before sending.

> They fret because they didn't get everything on their to-do list done this week.

> Then proceed to beat themselves up for not being perfect.

> They never launch a new program in their business because they aren't sure if it will be perfect.

The person running this strategy has rules that say:

> If it is perfect, I'm a good person.

> If it's not perfect, I'm in trouble and a bad person.

Usually they will have learnt that at school. Think back to your school days—perfection was most likely lavishly rewarded with love, praise and attention, especially if you were the "perfect child."

This strategy often presents itself in a perfectionist as intense stress, especially when they enter a new life situation rife with pressure to finish tasks quickly. The stress and fear can become so much that a perfectionist literally becomes paralysed with fear.

IF THIS IS YOU: WHAT TO DO

Nature teaches us how to be. Just check the weather. For how many days of the year is the weather absolutely perfect? How often are the waves at a surf beach absolutely perfect for surfing?

The answer is that sometimes they are, but mostly they are not. And anyway, the definition of perfect is completely different for each person. You might consider the perfect wave to be short, steep and fast, whereas I think the perfect wave is long, slow and easy to ride.

You really need to attack your mission headfirst, get your hands dirty, and FUCK IT UP. Make plenty of mistakes, because if you wait for conditions to be perfect, you will be waiting a hell of a long time.

As Reid Hoffman, the founder of LinkedIn.com, said at his

SxSW 2011 talk, "If you look back and are not completely embarrassed by your version 1.0, then you waited too long to launch it."

Get out there! Go do your thing! Have a go and get feedback— that is ultimately the path of the hero.

THE SUPER ACHIEVER STRATEGY

You may be thinking, but Dave, isn't that the whole point? To achieve outrageous results? Yes, indeed it is. But for what purpose?

You might see the super achiever pushing themselves to bigger and bigger accomplishments. They are relentlessly busy at the business of achieving—starting new businesses, buying more properties, training harder, going to every social engagement.

Society praises the super achiever for being incredible. "How does he do it all?" they will say. But, though he is doused with praise and admiration he is not fulfilled on the inside. In fact, he feels empty, as though his success is for nothing.

> *The hero gets a big raise. The feeling is not what he thought it would be.*

> *His business goes IPO. But still feels empty.*

He just ran his first marathon and no one saw him do it. The buzz is just not there.

He has an amazing family but just isn't happy.

He starts to freak out and stress and worry, and ask questions like, "What's wrong with me? Why don't I feel good? I <u>should</u> feel good. Am I a bad person?"

This pattern, if left unchecked, tailspins into a world of tension and frustration. No matter what the hero does, he can't get the feeling of happiness and fulfillment he wants. Eventually, he may start to feel sad and hopeless (or angry and frustrated), begin to give up on his dreams and lower his standards. "What's the point?" becomes his primary question.

<u>IF THIS IS YOU</u>: WHAT TO DO

Firstly, clarity is the key to change. If you can understand why this pattern is occurring, you can take back the power to change it. So let's begin peeling back the layers and see where this behaviour came from.

Typically, the hero will learn this pattern from a very young age and then it will be reinforced at school. For some reason, when he's young, the child feels as though they are inadequate or not good enough. Maybe they got teased at school for having big ears or a funny haircut. Or maybe there was a family secret that they had to cover up (because if anyone found out, it would bring shame to the family).

Whatever the original event, the child decides they have something to hide. So, because the pain of being found out would be too much to bear, they overcompensate for the feeling of inadequacy by being a super achiever. The achievements cover up the internal feeling of inadequacy, as everyone else is solely focused on the achievements. The child develops an internal rule that they will only be loved and significant when they are achieving at a high level.

At the deepest level, the super achiever's reason for pushing themselves to achieve is to GET admiration and love from people around them.

The ultimate purpose behind their achievements could be far more sustainable, if their intention was to instead GIVE love. Contributing to others is the key path to fulfillment.

The hero who falls into this pattern can immediately arrest it and begin to feel better by taking some time to rejuvenate their body. A day by the beach, a holiday, a massage, having some fun, being still (and feeling okay with that) are all ways that the super achiever can continue to achieve, while feeling recharged at the same time.

THE SITTING ON THE FENCE STRATEGY

After the hero accepts the initial call to adventure, he may find himself again caught at the crossroads. The difference is that this time, it's a higher quality problem.

He has a great idea for an iPhone app that he should start.

There is this awesome product that he thinks is ideal to drop ship.

He would go overseas and play sport.

He would launch an online business.

He could write a book.

Oh, and he also has his feet in three network marketing schemes. This is great, but how many of them are really progressing?

When people ask him, what do you do? - he has no idea how to answer because a short one-liner would take seven minutes to explain. This hero is often in the early, excited entrepreneur stage, where everything is a possibility.

The thing is, not a lot is actually being finished.

Pretty soon, the hero realises that he need to finish something so he can ship it and make the money. But then he has real trouble deciding which path to take. As time goes by, he gets more and more frustrated, and starts to become the guy who is "all talk and no walk."

<u>IF THIS IS YOU</u>: WHAT TO DO

Make a decision!

You need to recognise that struggling to decide which path to take is a classic sign of procrastination, or a fear of taking responsibility. Making a decision would mean having to take responsibility for making or creating an outcome, which could mean hard work. This is scary for some people. It's also going to keep you stuck.

As the hero, you need to pick a direction to go in. The most outrageous heroes make more decisions in a day than most people do in a year. If they get off track, they can quickly recalibrate and get back on track.

THE AVERAGE PERSON

    Makes decisions slowly.

    Changes their mind quickly.

THE HERO

    Makes decisions quickly.

    Changes their mind slowly.

When making a decision about which way to go, the hero will use the three-step formula used by Sir Richard Branson, Donald Trump, and Robert Kiyosaki:

What is the absolute worst-case scenario?

Is this acceptable to me? Could I handle the worst case?

If yes—proceed immediately. If no—decline and move on to the next decision.

Using this process is useful for reducing fear, because once you know what the worst case is, it suddenly becomes far easier to manage.

MODELING EXCELLENCE TO CREATE OUTRAGEOUS RESULTS

At every point of the Living Outrageously Hero's Journey, just prior to breaking through to the new world, the hero will usually undergo some type of special training to prepare for the challenges ahead. For example, the brand new entrepreneur buys books, goes to seminars and hires a coach to help them through to the next level. You see it in all modern movies too—Neo trained extensively with Morpheus before engaging with saving the world in the Matrix, and Luke Skywalker met and trained with Obi Wan in Star Wars.

These examples have one thing in common: the up-and-coming hero has found a wise model from which to gain new tools, strategies and techniques. And, while all of these things are key components, by far the most valuable component of this training is learning to apply the most effective thinking to a particular situation, in order to create the most outrageous result. When you model someone's thinking as well as how they did it, that is truly modeling excellence.

For example, you are overweight and your personal trainer gives you a meal plan and exercise regime. He has given you all the tools you need to be successful, but nothing will change unless the mindset shifts too. If you use food as a distraction from your boring life, or to fill up after you feel emotionally empty, you need to think about food in a new way in order to create the outrageous results you desire. Ask any person with a fit, trim, lean body what food means to them, and they will tell you: it's fuel. It's fuel to keep your human body operating at optimal function.

HOW DID YOU DO THAT?

Remember, there are seven billion people on this planet. Someone has solved your exact problem before. You just have to find them and ask how they did it.

"How did you do that?" This is the fundamental question that will uncover someone's strategy for a great result. Usually, the model will be very happy to tell you how they did it, as they will be proud to have contributed to your success.

Ask them for their process. Compare it to yours, and then fill in the gaps. You might find you are missing some large chunks of the process.

> *If you have a friend who is at 10% body fat and bench presses 100kg, ask him what he focuses on to make that happen.*

> *If you are closing 25% of sales appointments and your colleague is closing 85%, ask him how he does it.*

> *If your friends have an amazing, loving, passionate relationship, ask them what is important to them.*

And when you do notice your gaps, don't feel bad, feel excited. They are just gaps. And now you know what they are, you can close them.

THE SECRET FORMULA TO MODELLING EXCELLENCE

Now, in the majority of cases, this should be enough to decide the strategy you need to proceed on your Living Outrageously Hero's Journey. But for those of you who really want a comprehensive approach and find out exactly *how to model*—use this 7 Levels of Thinking framework.

To illustrate this model, I am going to use the example of how I ran a 100km ultra-marathon with only five months of preparation and having never run more than 10km before. In this case, I modeled a number of people, but mostly Tim Ferriss and Brian Mackenzie. I have never met either, but I identified with their strategy in the book, *The 4-Hour Body*.

IDENTITY: Identity is a key element. It's the "I am…" statement of who the person believes they are when they are doing that thing. This global belief is so important, because it often describes how they acted to challenges. Prior to entering the race, I would've said I couldn't run. I would've told you I am not a runner, but I am a rugby player. After reading Ferriss' book, it became clear I needed to switch my identity to that of an ultra-runner, even before I had done it. Since the key to successful modeling is to act as if you are the model, I accepted that belief.

Identity: I am an ultra-marathon runner.

For You - Ask Your Model

When you do [the thing], who are you?

What's your identity when you do [the thing]?

BELIEFS: The conventional belief is that you need to pound the pavement and rack up the miles to prepare for such a long event. You know, a mere 100km per week in training. Runners don't typically lift weights or do strength work either. Tim Ferriss' belief is different. He got his beliefs from his model of excellence, Brian Mackenzie, a fellow ultra-runner who had to find a shorter, more convenient way to train after his wife threatened to leave him if he was out running for 30 hours each week. With his marriage on the line, Mackenzie found a way to train for just six hours per week and still be fully prepared for the race. A mix of high intensity, cross-fit style workouts with a large strength component, it was completely different to the conventional beliefs.

What did I do?

I adopted Ferriss' and Mackenzie's beliefs as my own, and began to train just six hours per week. Remember, the key here is just to do as the model does. Do what they did and you will get the results they got. Why try to reinvent the wheel?

For You - Ask Your Model

What do you believe about [the thing]?

VALUES: Values are what is important to you when you are
doing each thing. Ferriss found cross-fit endurance expert Dr.
Kelly Starrett, who said that flexibility and mobility of the lower
limbs was massively important to the success of a first time
ultra-runner. "Focus on the flexibility," he said. So I did, and
began my daily ritual of stretching to prepare for the race.

For You - Ask Your Model

When you engage in [your thing], what is most important to you?
What do you focus on?

ENVIRONMENT: Our environment is a key indicator of our
success, or lack of success. You are the average of your five
closes friends in terms of income, happiness, and everything in
between. Ferriss says to get out into the mountains as much as
possible, to practise being out there. Get around the
environment that will best support your outcome.

So I did. I went to the bush every week for five months.

For You - Ask Your Model

*What type of people do you hang around with, to be successful at [the
thing]?*

Where is the best place in the world for [the thing]?

How should I best set up my home environment to be successful at [the thing]?

SKILLS/CAPABILITIES: Every great model will tell you the essential skills for creating success. In business, the major skills required are sales and marketing. Every business must have a strategy for this.

Every sporting team needs players of certain skills to execute an effective game. For this ultra, a couple of key skills were: 1) Running technique, especially downhill. 2) Management of nutrition and hydration throughout. A key marker of my capability to even start the training was being able to run 5km in 24 minutes or less.

For You - Ask Your Model

What are the 3 core skills I need to be successful at [the thing]?
What must I be proficient at to be successful?

MISSION: Ferriss' mission was to become superhuman. He wanted to prove that results could happen rapidly if you find the most effective strategy. The key here is to ask what the model is ultimately trying to do/achieve.

My mission was to inspire others to run.

For You - Ask Your Model

What's your mission when you engage in the thing?

OUTSTANDING MODELS OF EXCELLENCE

Below are some of world's best models of excellence, in their respective areas.

Marketing—Seth Godin, Frank Kern, Brendon Burchard

Sales—Chet Holmes

Success—Tony Robbins

Health—Tim Ferriss, Kelly Starrett, Brian Mackenzie, David Wolfe

Relationships—David Dieda, Marie Forleo, Alice Hammerlae

Personal Finance—Robert Kiyosaki

Leadership—Richard Branson

Spirituality—The Dalai Lama, Ester Hicks, Eckhart Tolle

FINAL THOUGHTS ON MODELING

Unconsciously, many of us will use our parents as a model.

Dad was a doctor, so you become a doctor. Mum liked nice clothes, so you like nice clothes. Dad got angry when he didn't get his own way, so you do the same. And that's all fine, until the anger you modeled off your dad starts to disrupt your Living Outrageously Hero's Journey. Remember, nothing is good or bad unless you make it so.

My only question to you is: how is that working for you?

CHAPTER SIXTEEN
ENJOY A FULL EXPERIENCE OF LIFE

"Everyday, when I wake up, I am torn between two desires, to help the world, and to enjoy the world."

— Warren Miller

The hero knows that he has limited time on Earth. If he lives to be 80, he only has about 18,000 days left (if he is currently 30). He knows that there are many great causes and many great opportunities for him to use his skills to contribute to the life of others. He also enjoys his freedom and desires a life full of amazing, enjoyable experiences. Snorkeling with the dolphins in Hawaii is awesome, after all!

But sometimes, in his desire to have it all and live an outrageous life, he mistakenly forms the view that his work and his play are in direct opposition to one another, and that he must choose. Of course, this is all just a made-up belief designed to keep him safe from having a full experience of life.

As a life coach, I see it play out in clients who say things like:

"I hate my job, but I need money. I wish I could go partying more often."

"I like my job, but all I ever do is work. I never have any fun."

"No one ever takes me seriously because they think I am crazy."

"If only I could save $1 million, then I could retire."

Comments like this show me they have an internal conflict.

```
FREEDOM                RESPONSIBILITY
  FUN          VS.          WORK
  KID                       ADULT
```

Clients will tend to fall into one of these two categories, and that is causing them pain. We need to integrate them both so you can have the perfect amount of both in your life. The most common pattern I see is the client who is rebelling (being the kid) against the need to be responsible and work. I know I certainly did this pattern for a number of years. I was angry at being "made" to work in a law firm, and I didn't want to! I wanted to travel the world, play rugby, ski and see the sights.

But this was my mistake: I was forcing myself to take responsibility for a life and journey that I didn't want to take. Something inside my soul told me that I was not meant to be a lawyer, that I was destined for greater things. The lawyer path was a path I had fallen into—not a direction that I had consciously chosen.

Here is the breakthrough realisation:

YOU ONLY HAVE TO TAKE RESPONSIBILITY FOR DOING THE THING YOU WERE PUT HERE TO DO.

In my heart, I felt like I was put here to inspire people to live a happy, healthy and successful life. I couldn't see how the vehicle of being a lawyer was going to drive me to that destination. When I did eventually take responsibility for consciously creating my Living Outrageously Hero's Journey, I found a new vehicle of coaching, and I knew it was right for me.

I knew it was right because my whole energy lifted and my enthusiasm transformed the instant I was in the coaching environment, around other coaches and discussing coaching challenges. I was thirsty for knowledge on every coaching subject, and I could not get enough.

Plus it met my criteria.

Will this vehicle allow me to help people live a great life? Yes.

Will this vehicle offer me the opportunity to make unlimited money? Yes.

Are there role models ahead of me, who I aspire to be? Yes.

Does this environment feel like where I was meant to be? Yes.

Does this feel like what I was meant to do, what I was put here to do? Yes.

These are some great questions to ask yourself when considering whether to engage with a new vehicle in your journey. Because when you ask these questions, you are taking responsibility for your journey, not Uncle Tom's pre-determined path for you.

And on the other side of the journey, the ultimate gift of true freedom will be yours to experience.

People think freedom is winning a big sum of money and sitting on the beach for the rest of their life. That might be fun for a while, but it won't lead you to true fulfillment. The only way to feel truly fulfilled is to sharing your gifts with others.

So start giving your gift.

Do what you do.

DO WHAT YOU WERE PUT HERE TO DO

Pretty early on in my legal career, I started looking around for mentors who I could look up to. I was looking for someone who led me to say, "YES! This person is a role model for me. I want to be that person when I get older."

I looked and looked and looked, but never found someone in the field of law that I aspired to be. All the partners were fat, unfit, unhealthy, worked long hours and had poor relationships with their wives. I didn't want that.

I wanted love, passion, health, fun, success, happiness and contribution. So the very second I walked into a Tony Robbins seminar in 2011 and experienced the health, happiness and positive energy there, I knew I had found my crowd.

Finding your crowd and the appropriate vehicle for expressing yourself in work is critical to your success on the Living Outrageously Hero's Journey. Until you find these things, you will may be isolated, alone and miserable.

CHOOSE EFFECTIVE VEHICLES

One of Tony Robbins' teachings is that the purpose of life is to find as many vehicles for fulfilling your needs as possible. Notice how he says many vehicles, not just one.

This is where I see many of clients run into pain:

> *Their partner leaves and their world falls apart permanently.*

> *They get injured and can't play their favourite sport anymore.*

> *Something happens and they lose their job, think they will never get a job as good.*

Sure, when things happen, it is human nature to want to grieve the loss of that vehicle. But, like everything, you have a choice about how to react.

You could stay sad forever. Thinking you have lost a part of you, and are now somehow incomplete, not good enough, or broken.

Or you could realize that you were always whole, and that while it's sad this vehicle has had to move on, in time you can find a new vehicle for meeting your needs.

This pattern has halted the progress of many hero journeys, when someone just can't get over a breakup or other major life event.

Hopefully, now that you are aware of it, you can move forward on your journey and find new vehicles for experiencing your great desires.

ENJOY THE WORLD

"I wish I had worked more hours."

- Said no one. Ever.

The world is a huge place full of spectacular treasures. Whatever you are into, there are many magnificent experiences out there just waiting for you.

In 2006, I was heli-skiing in the Kootenays in British Columbia. It was a beautiful bluebird day, and my dream to one day go heli-skiing was finally being realised. We had completed our allotted number of runs for the day early, and seeing as the weather was magic, the chopper pilot asked if we would like to do some more runs. But it would be $90 each. And everyone had to agree.

Before any of us could even speak, Cameron, the father figure of the group (he was 30 years old) shouted to the pilot that of course, we would go again. This shocked the group a little—he was so forward and he hadn't consulted anyone.

But what Cameron said next was pure inspiration:

"The majority of us sit at a desk all day, all year, and about the most
exciting thing that happens is that the boss leaves early so we get to leave
early too. And here we are, in the middle of freaking nowhere, in a
freaking helicopter, with a group of awesome people, it's sunny outside and
the powder is fresh and deep. How often do you get a chance to experience
that? Of course, we are doing the run!!"

And with that, the group cheered and off we went, for two
more runs, and so we really milked the day for all it had, going
to sleep content that we had maximised our experience of life
that day.

THE 457

When I was 23, I asked myself an important question: When
money is no longer an issue for you and you don't need to
work, what will you do with all your free time?

Though quite a confident question to ask, it prompted me to
think about my bucket list. So I wrote and wrote and wrote, as
my ideas began to pour out of me. I thought about all the
outrageous adventures and activities that I would love to do.

At the completion of my writing frenzy, I had written down
457 activities or adventures that I would like to participate in. I
call it my 457. I wrote:

All the physical challenges I wanted to complete: marathons, representative teams, and how much I'd bench press.

The treks I'd take: Everest Base Camp, Kilimanjaro, Machu Picchu.

The fish I'd catch: marlin and salmon.

The people I'd meet: Arnie, Bill Clinton and Bart Simpson.

The concerts I'd go to: AC/DC and Black Eyed Peas.

The philanthropic work I'd do: build a school.

The documentaries I'd produce: 52 sports in 52 countries in 52 weeks.

The people I would coach: presidents, musicians and Olympic athletes.

The dance moves I want to master: breakdancing and crumping.

The inspiration I felt at the end of this brainstorming session was amazing. I had given further definition to why and what I was aiming for on my Living Outrageously Hero's Journey

ACTIVITY: CREATE YOUR OWN 457

So now it's your turn to write your 457.

Grab a little notebook and start writing!

Where do you want to travel?

Who do you want to meet?

What do you want to give?

What quirky/funny activities would make you happy?

What physical challenges do you want to complete?

What new hobbies could you take up?

Gratitude For The Reader

Before closing this book, I want to personally thank you, the reader, for trusting me to be your guide on this hero's journey. I appreciate you. I know you are out there, on the path, taking action everyday to move towards your outrageous destination. I know your heart is full of good intentions for making the world a better place, and I want to honour that in you.

Thank you too, for being a part of my journey as an author, coach and speaker.

You've got all the tools you need to be the hero.

So go. It's your time!

Live Outrageously.

Dave

P.S. I love email, especially from fellow hero's on the path. If you feel called to do so, send me a note, sharing how you are going on your hero's journey. I'd love to hear from you.

dave@livingoutrageously.com

Acknowledgements

There are so many people I would like to thank for helping me get this book to market. As anyone who has ever thought about writing a book knows, it can seem like a daunting task when you first set out. I have been fortunate to have an amazing support team around me.

To my wonderful partner Susan Santoro, your encouragement and support has meant everything to me and I appreciate the space you gave me to retreat to the man cave to produce this book.

To my parents, Steve & Kathy, who probably freaked out the moment I told them I was quitting law to become a life coach, thank you for showing faith in me.

To my main man, co-creator of The Living Outrageously Podcast, Matt "the freakin' man" Kelly, I salute you. If you had not brought your unique perspective, living outrageously would never have taken off. Thank you sincerely.

To my mentors – Alice Hammerlae, Sharon Pearson, Joe Pane, Jonnie Cass, Tony Robbins, Seth Godin, Tim Ferris, Gary Vaynerchuk – thank you for walking the path first, and showing me the light. Your contribution is worth its weight in gold.

To Michele Jones, whose houseboat retreat invitation sparked the fire for this revised edition. Thank you to the end of the world and back. You are an inspiration.

And finally, to all the dedicated viewers of the Living Outrageously Podcast. Without your loyal support, the concept would never have gone as big as it did.

Thank you, and may your life be as outrageous as you desire.

About The Author – Dave Thompson

Dave Thompson is the founder of The SpiritCast Network, a company that helps entrepreneurs profit from passionately sharing their message with the world. His company offers Breakthrough Business Coaching Programs, Create Your #1 Podcast trainings, and their very popular "Inspirational Book Writers Retreat" where you spend a week in a tropical island paradise, write your book, and then have it published 6 weeks later.

He loves tropical islands, coconuts, and spending time with his fiancé Susan.

About Business Breakthrough Coaching Programs

"I went from zero to $1million in my business in 10 months, and I just bought my own house, with a waterfall in the backyard" – Josh Newton, Breakthrough Coaching Client

I work personally with an exclusive number of private clients each year, assisting them to breakthrough to success in their business and personal life so they can be an inspiration to others.

If you resonated with the message and this book and would like to chat with me about becoming a client, send me an email and we can schedule a confidential, complimentary chat J

dave@livingoutrageously.com

About The Inspirational Book Writers Retreat

Come To Paradise For A Week – Be Published 6 Weeks Later

"An amazing step that is without question a game changer"
– Danijela Mijic, August 2014

Four times a year, we invite an exclusive group of business owners to the tropical paradise of North Stradbroke Island, off the coast of Queensland, Australia to participate in a very special event. The offer is very simple, come to paradise for a week, complete your manuscript, and we take care of the publishing so you will be published in 6 weeks.

This event is aimed at entrepreneurs, small business owners, coaches, consultants or personal brands that want to publish a book to become an expert authority in their industry. It has been said that a book gives your business magical powers in terms of positioning and ability to charge premium prices.

We know that life as an entrepreneur is often hectic and fast paced, and that's why we take care of everything that has been stopping you from completing your book:

- Our comprehensive pre-retreat preparation phase helps you overcome the biggest problem many face – that of getting started

- You get to join a group of like-minded individuals on the same mission as you, in an environment set up for creative success. The distractions of the modern world do not even exist here on the island.

- We take care of many the bits and pieces that make your book – we handle the entire publishing side of things for you.

If you are interested, get in contact with me directly and we can schedule a complimentary chat about your book. Send me an email now and we can get chatting J

dave@livingoutrageously.com

Find Dave Online

Public Figure Profile page on Facebook:

https://www.facebook.com/AUSDaveThompson

Personal Profile on Facebook:

http://www.facebook.com/DavoDome

Instagram: http://instagram.com/thedavethompson

Website: http://www.davethompson.com.au/

DAVE'S NEXT BOOK – Released in 2015

"BALANCE After Burnout"

Due for release in 2015, Dave's next book, "Balance After Burnout" examines burnout along the entrepreneurial journey.

Why do we wear busy-ness as a badge of honour?

Why does it feel so hard to keep in-balance, and live a balanced life?

Dave presents his revolutionary, world first methodology called the "Axis of Balance", which is a simple, self checking system that anyone can use in a matter of minutes to determine where they are out of balance, and what to do about it.

If you have not been feeling good, are grinding out a living financially or struggling to maintain passion and purpose in your relationships and business, this book will change your life.

Available 2015 in the Kindle, iBooks and Amazon.

www.ingramcontent.com/pod-product-compliance
Lightning Source LLC
Chambersburg PA
CBHW070907180526
45168CB00005B/1961